Abiding Love

By

Vernon D. Lloyd
With
Shaunta Ellis

Abiding Love

Copyright 2024
Vernon D. Lloyd

No part of this book may be reproduced or transmitted in any form or by any means electronic, or mechanical, including photocopying and recording, or by any information storage or retrieval system, without permission from the author.

All Rights Reserved

Cover Design by FreePix,com

A Vernon Lloyd Ministries Production

In Memory of:

DaddyClaude Ellis
Pastor Lee Hunter
Deacon Harold De Loach
Deacon Harvey Holloway Sr.
Deacon George Neal, Sr.
Deacon Clymon Tanner, Sr.
Deacon Clarence Brown
Deacon James R. Barnes
Deacon Burrell McCollum, Sr.
Brother Otis Odom

Dedication

Brother Edward Ellis
&
Pastor Gregory Thomas

Introduction

Every morning is a new day is as a fresh page in a journal. It lies before us blank waiting for us to fill it with ideas and happenings. It waits for our experiences, wishes and dreams. It is the vehicle that bears our history from generation to generation allowing those who never met us to know us and better understand who they are and where we have been. That page is a well of refreshing for them to draw from and for us to relive and draw daily inspiration.

Every morning provides a new opportunity to live life in a fuller manner. It is a challenge to make deposits as well as set agendas for the future. From the time we hit the floor *(not literally)* we face a world of opportunity and obstacle. We need the courage and inspiration to go forth without fear. We need reminders that the great God of the universe is with us and seeks to help us navigate our paths. His presence is not only one of power but an inexhaustible source of love that abides with us. His assurance of this is abiding is clearly taught by him in John chapter 15 and that continuing presence in Matthew 28:20.

The intent in this 40 day devotional is not to provide deep theological thought but to provide kindling to start your day. It is to help jumpstart your thinking and give you courage and faith not only to face the world but make a difference knowing that such action is an expression of God's love. It is for you to spark a conversation with God and be reminded of a love that is with you not only to have but to share in the lives of others.

You only need a moment in the course of your day to read each devotional. It would go well with prayer time, morning devotion, coffee, breakfast or any other moment to start your day. There is nothing like hearing God say I love you and living in the daily assurance that the love he shares is for us to abide in forever. I pray this work will bless you with every reading.

Shaunta Ellis

"As the Father has loved me, so have I loved you. Now abide in my love. If you obey my commands, you will abide in my love just as I have obeyed my Father's commands and abide in his love" ~ *John 15:9 – 10*

Abiding Love
Day 1

Good Morning,

This is my question to you as you start your day. Why am I being nosey? I am not. Inquiring minds just want to know. What are you going to do with this day? I just want to give you something to think of. You have been given this day. Do not miss its value. You have 24 fresh hours, 1440 minutes and 86,400 seconds available to you. Do not waste them. Put the best of you into them. Spend them better than you do a dollar; for money spent can be gained again, but a moment once spent can never be reclaimed. Enjoy your time and invest it. Live it so well that God will want to grant you more days because you make so much out of them.

Do not just let them pass. Like vegetables on your plate with parents looking over your shoulder, you know it's best for you to eat them all. They may not be your most delightful thing to eat, but they help make life so much better. Think about my question and make it happen. You have 24 fresh hours...Live them! Much Love!

Abiding Love
Day 2

Good Morning,

Indeed, it is just that, simply because it is. Let us view each day as God did when he created them. He paused and took a step back. He looked at each day and said, "It is good." That included the evening and the morning. Did you know that the reason he did that was that every day he did something special? He had a plan for it. He would not leave it as a blank canvas but wanted to leave his mark upon it.

Think it through. What are you going to do with this good day? Are you going to randomly live or make a mark? It is good to just do something, but it is better to have a plan. See it with clear eyes. Give it great thought. See the benefits, costs, obstacles and sacrifices you will have to make. Understand how the ceiling for this day becomes the floor for the one to follow. Write down that plan.

Put it to work and do not abandon it. Adjust if you must. Share it with someone but make certain you retain ownership. Work it out and enjoy doing so. You are the one! Dream it then pursue it. That sounds like a plan. Have a plan, do-it day and when it ends, be able to say, "It was good." Much Love!

Abiding Love
Day 3

Good Morning,

It is a good day to initiate this practice: Claim what you do well and admit what you do not. Truthfulness to self builds confidence. It also reduces the stress of trying to pass yourself as someone you are not and that you may not even like. Be free to be you. Do not permit others to define you nor determine what you can and cannot be. Tell yourself there will be no masquerading today.

It is just as important to admit what you do not do well and do not desire to be. Other's expectations should not drive one to create a personal type of Oz. Place a premium on authenticity and truth. It is better to become more of who you are than to seek to add who you are not.

Share yourself with pride. Present those great parts. It is okay to own and declare your greatness. There's no humility in denying your truth. You rob others of what is great in you. Only you have the opportunity to be the very best YOU; therefore, get to work. Practice makes perfect. The world needs the best YOU... Go ahead and do it. Go ahead and be it. Have a do-li-shus day. Much Love!

Abiding Love
Day 4

Good Morning,

Remember those days after the grill was fired up and meat seemed to be laid in sacrifice. Do you remember when the smoke went up from it like incense and all you could think of was getting a paper plate, a fork, a knife and a place to devour that sacrifice doused with Sweet Baby Rays and Lawry's Seasoning Salt? Those were the days. Someone would ask the next day, "Are you taking that rib sandwich to work?" You could not hide the grease coming through the brown paper bag and just said, "Uh huh" with no thought of stopping or sharing. I submit that leftovers from the holidays are cool.

You probably have had some potato salad and baked beans with hamburgers and burnt hot dogs too. That is good eating. Food, like sweet tea, tends to get better the next day. So do many life experiences. Just because you had it yesterday does not mean it loses flavor or substance and is not good today. It does not mean you consumed all to be had when it came off the grill... Savor the good times. Put them in a takeout container. Revisit and reopen. You may need to create some more just like them. You have the recipe. You have mastered the process and can create moments and experiences that delight your taste for life. In the words of a song from my long-gone teen years, "Do it 'til you're satisfied"; (Make certain it is a good thing).

By the way...if you are not going to eat that chicken

thigh in the refrigerator, I can make a sandwich with it that will make Chick- Fil-A and Zaxby's cry. Okay!
Oh, you going to have another leftover tonight? Be that way! (LOL) Have a beautiful day. Much Love!

Abiding Love
Day 5

Good Morning,

Let us be mindful of Memorial Day. Enjoy the time shared, the events, the grilling and all else in which we culturally engage. However, let us be mindful that the true meaning of the day is remembrance of those who have sacrificed life for their country. Let us not permit the time off and the delicious festive food offerings cause us to forget the honorees to be celebrated.

Blood is not cheap and in memory should not be discounted. We are able to live as we do because of the service and sacrifice of so many men and women whose names may never find a marquee or receive formal recognition. That blood is not one type. It is a blood coming from and combined of a variety of ethnic, socio-economic, religious, political and gender blood. It is honorable and to be solemnly celebrated thoughtfully and reverently. With every visit you make to a cemetery, it is not out of line to pass through the alumni chapter of American heroes and give a salute. Heroes may die, but their acts live forever. Pause and celebrate a veteran who paid the ultimate price for our freedom. That person is certainly worthy. Much Love!

Abiding Love
Day 6

Good Morning,

Have you ever felt like someone poured molasses or that thick sweet syrup in your life's tank? That once fired up high octane, clean burning self becomes bogged, and you seem to need a flush. Sometimes our lives become sluggish, and we move slowly (such was my case). This is often not by choice. There is a place called stuck that we all find from time to time, and although we have some motion, it is like that of the aforementioned molasses.

Stuck renders our spiritual lives drained and we become negatively impacted. We try to drive ourselves out of it only to find that we have created a deep groove, and our wheels are just spinning. Weariness sets in but do not succumb to it. This is so easy. It is understood. Everyone does it from time to time. Isn't that, right? It is so normal. Do not let it be the norm for you. Do not sulk or wade in weariness. Get some help. You do not have to do it alone. Ruts are best overcome when someone is there to help you out. Refresh and restore vitality. Know when to rest and do not let an unhealthy condition control your day. Time spent with those we love is too important to spend it in less than optimum condition.

It is good to speak to your significant special self. Thank you for being a motivation and a friend. Well, off to worship my good friend! Much Love!

Abiding Love
Day 7

Good Morning,

Walk like you are going somewhere because you are doing just that today. Put on your good shoes and take some good steps. Capture your stride and let the rhythm in your walk announce to the world that you are coming. The world is your runway. You are somebody! Do not slump, drag your feet or hold your head down. Quicken your step and extend your stride.

Speak to yourself and let your legs and feet broadcast the affirmations in your conversation. Set your eyes forward and establish your step so solidly that you leave footprints for others to follow. You invite your company by how you walk. Those content with "right here" will be passed and left behind. Only if you are going nowhere can you hang in the same place with anyone, but if you have your step, stride and shoes for walking, you must say, "no" to even friends and loved ones issuing invitations to stand still. Life is best moved in motion, and though busy can be an enemy to blessed, moving in purpose keeps you strong and makes life meaningful.

When it becomes necessary to stand still, let it be in the same character as your walk. Own who you are and testify of it. Let us hit the road and do it. We have some footprints to make. Remember that the world is your runway. Walk it! Have a Swag and Sway kind of day. Much Love!

Abiding Love
Day 8

Good Morning,

I hope today is just dandy in its beginning for you. *Did I say, "Dandy?"* It seems you need a little something this morning. If you are like me a great cup of coffee would be nice. How about one of those breakfasts that is like morning feasts? A day off would work well and a pass entitling you to 8 more hours of premium sleep with no interruptions (including bathroom runs) would have us doing the Snoopy dance. I would love to give all those to you, but I do not have them in my hand or pocket. I do, however, have something wrapped I want to leave with you this morning with hope that you will also share with someone.

I want to issue this gift to you simply because I want you to have it. I do not have tons of money (a few extra pounds would be good) but I offer you love and support as you go forth. You are going to get this love. I am bringing it through the door and placing it on the table. I am here to support you. This is how I do it; I am here to love with the best love. It is my desire to love well and although I have by no means perfected it, I strive every day. Please receive this from me. I truly want you to have it and invite you to give to others this gift I offer you. There is no bill on the table; Have a wonderful day. Much Love!

Abiding Love
Day 9

Good Morning,

Do you remember growing up and hearing your dad say, "Speak up so someone can hear you?" Mom would admonish you to not bring all that loudness in the house and use your inside voice. Church Mothers would admonish you in a nice tone with the possibility of judgment present to speak in whispers; God can hear you and so can others. You had to be aware of what you were saying and where you were. Those directing our vocality taught us that volumes may not be the same, but you will be heard if you speak in a way that those listening can hear. Therefore speak!

It is good to make your voice heard. It is not good to sit back and take it all in when you have something necessary to say. Speak up! Do not wait for others to read your mind or always say it on your behalf. It may not be communicated. Please understand; I am not suggesting being belligerent and rude. I do not suggest hollering and screaming. Speak up! Yours is a needed voice in a world needing true dialogue. Do not be silent and let the world ignore you or drown out your sound.

Everyone will not be listening but do not let that stymie your voice. Communicate, say, "amen", nod your head, wave a hand, use a thumb, write a note, vote, show affection, live with passion and get it out. Sing your song in the chorus of life. Doing so makes the song much better. Speak up! People are listening. Have a good day. Much Love!

Abiding Love
Day 10

Good Morning,

I have a question for you again. *(Why are you giving me the side eye?)* I know it is early but let me put something on your mind and in your spirit. Are you ready? Okay! What do you want to give and what do you desire to give today? I think that is a great consideration and if thought through can impact every day that you live. Are those answers stacking up? Okay, what is your answer? I hope you are thinking, "I want to give and receive the best."

Let this be your desire. Mediocre is easy. Good is better but why not shoot for best. When you do you raise your standards of living as well as your expectations of others. You live on a higher plane and the altitude will impact your behavior and engagements with others. Let's keep it simple today. I do not wish the basics, the good or the bad, but the BEST for you.
B... Beautiful
E... Excellent
S... Strong
T... True
Anything less is not intended for you. Let the world know it is coming from you. Prepare to receive it. Have a great day. I wish you the best. Much Love!

"Place me like a seal over your heart, like a seal on your arm; for love is as strong as death, its jealousy unyielding as the grave. It burns like a blazing fire" ~ Song of Solomon 8:6

Abiding Love
Day 11

Good Morning,

Take it easy today. Some folks say that just to say it, but I do not. I mean more. My admonition is more than a loosely tossed around word. We all need to relax. We do not need to be stressing. All that does is raise your blood pressure and diminish your good looks. If something arises that you can handle then do so. If you cannot handle it, call for reinforcements and leave it alone until you can manage it.

Take a deep breath and take life as it comes.
Stressing does not bring blessing, and worry gives you nothing. Over-thinking will not make you think better, and reflecting on the past too much does not make you ready for the future. Get it as life gives it and do the best you can with it.

Take it easy. Do not burden yourself with the trivial. Get up under it without allowing it to crush you. Wait! Be ready for it when it comes. Am I making sense? Okay! Handle your day and all that's in it. Everything may not be easy, but take your time, and even the hard things get done. Have a day in His peace. Much Love!

Abiding Love
Day 12

Good Morning,

A story from my recent past serves as the base of what we will reflect on this morning. I had one of the best cups of coffee. It tasted so good; I kept shaking it to be certain I had not left a drop of it. I thanked that cup and the persons that had filled it. I almost mourned as the last drops saturated my throat with coffee drinker's pleasure. I kept the cup for some time and after a while, I dropped it. I picked it up without panic. A co-worker panicked at my casual retrieval until he realized my cup was empty. He looked at me and asked, "Why are you carrying an empty paper coffee cup?"

A simple but profound thought came to mind. Why am I walking around with empty purposeless things? The cup used to hold something meaningful, but now that it is gone, what was my purpose? I was carrying emptiness. My friend's question stirred me. What else was I holding onto that no longer had purpose? Are you in the same boat?

Do not hold on to things just because you have had them. If it serves no further purpose, it is time to either let it go or recycle it. If it is not good for you, stop it.
You may have even become comfortable giving yourself and being less than good. It is a bad habit. Stop it! It may not be easy, but stop. Skid if you must, but stop. When you stop, you can get started on what is good for you. A fresh cup of both life and coffee awaits you as

soon as you release and lay aside the empty ones. Refills are available. Much Love!

Abiding Love
Day 13

Good Morning,

It is always good to take time and say "I love you". It does not matter the time of day or what your schedule might be. It is but a three word phrase, yet the potency it possesses is amazing. Say it and mean it. Rehearse it and be certain you say it well. Be certain you have the right tone and object of your profession.

The ear responds to the spoken word, therefore, never think because you said it yesterday, it is good for today. Fresh words are like fresh water and fresh bread. Be convincing. Move beyond moods and circumstances. Say it going and returning; it is a great investment in others. It costs nothing that you do not already have, therefore, release it and receive. God will stock you well because this is the most important thing we can do for each other in His sight. He tells us to love him and to love our neighbor as ourselves. That is a command! Why not let the words speak clearly today?

Do not go out without spreading the love today. You have your assignment; *(Can I do that? Can I give assignments?).* Well, until a verdict comes back, I will stand on that admonition. The word for this is: "du-it-tu-it-lak-u-nu-*it'* *(Do it to it like you knew it).* Have a great day. I am leaving right now and saying to you Much Love!

Abiding Love
Day 14

Good Morning,

On your mark, get set, go! The race is on and the prize awaits the winner at the finish line. You want to win. No one should try to lose, but that is the probability if one does not prepare to win. Preparation and practice are essential. They give you stamina and strategy for when it is your time to step forward.

Be ready when opportunity comes. Before you can go where you want, you have to be where you need to be and fit for the journey. You cannot wish yourself there. You must do some things. You must prepare. You must pack. You must position yourself. You cannot catch a flight, train or cruise. You do not look for a cruise in the desert or a plane in a dense wooded area. You must be at the right place at the right time with the right provision to make the trip. Be willing to pay the cost and move from here to there so you will be ready. Be ready to go even though you do not know when the time of departure may be.

Whether your trip is physical, geographical or spiritual, you must prepare and move. Do not miss what you so want because you were not ready when opportunity knocked. I am continuing a journey as we speak so I am moving. Opportunity might be outside right now. Grasp it! Have an "ex-er-ci-zing-mo-by-scoo-ta-bout-da" *(exercising mobile scoot about' day)*. Much Love!

Abiding Love
Day 15

Good Morning...

Get excited about something or someone, and let it be known. Be careful not to get out the wrong side of the bed. If you declare that you are not a morning person, stop that right now. Am I sounding too bossy? Let me rephrase it: Stop wrecking your morning. New things await you and a poor attitude towards yourself and the day can mess that up.

Quit mumbling! Think of everything you can thank or ask God for. Think of possibilities that can happen with peace, joy and optimism. Rock bottom means there is no way, but up, and when you have reached the top, the only way is onward. Celebrate with passion and raise your voice and hands. Say it loud...so loud in fact that someone wants to know "Hey, what is going on with you?" Then go ahead and tell them. Get them involved. No one can get excited over what and who is meaningful to you if you do not.

Look in the mirror at yourself sometimes and get excited. Turn a few heads. Make some noise. Be number one in your own book, and be willing to cheer others in your life the same way. Today I am celebrating you in the same manner as above. I got my hands in the air. I wave them like I just don't care *(not original but you get the point...I hope)*. Go on with your bad self! Live your life like it's golden. Go Kool N the Gang on everyone and celebrate!

, you have your orders and I am out of breath.
Have a cheer-n- oooh-U ba-bee-X-2- sho--ya-rat da *(cheering oooh baby baby sho" you right day)*. The Lord may have to deliver me from wild vocabulary. Much Love!

Abiding Love
Day 16

Good Morning...

Whatever you set out to do is possible. Do not let history talk you out of it. Because it has not happened does not mean it cannot happen. You may be the origin and the original. Imagination transcends what is and gives birth to new creations. There may be a model or there may be nothing but what you dream or see. In any case, get to work.

Bend your knees; put your shoulder to it; pull and lift. Succeed, fail, correct and perfect. You may need a little lineament, but you can do it. It may be hard, but it does not make it impossible, and you are the parent of it.
 I am a cheerleader in your destiny.

No criticism or commentary. You might be doing something that may change the world or show us how to do something a better way. You may be teaching that more than one person can do it and how to make it happen in different places and circumstances. I declare, "You can do it!" Much Love!

Abiding Love
Day 17

Good Morning....

You were made to be a lover. Yep! So if you are cold without care or passion, you are living outside of your created intent. You cannot just mother love. Love cannot be at its best unless you exercise it. It is not a mere emotion. It is not an elevated state of kindness. It is divine. It is of God. It is the most potent force on the earth, but it is never at its best until it is exercised and built.

Practice it when no one asks for it. Practice it towards those who like you as well as those who do not. Practice when you go before God. Let Him show you how to love yourself and Him. If you can love yourself and see yourself through the loving eyes of God, you can love and see others the same way. Refuse to hate and when others hurt, fail or disappoint you, respond with love.

I am not crazy! I saw you roll your eyes. The best lovers go through it. If you truly love you will have achieved your first objective. If it is not received right away you may be disappointed, but you know: (1) it was what you desired to do and give and (2) it never fails. Have a loving day. Much Love!

Abiding Love
Day 18

Good Morning,

Take time to pray. Stop right there! Did you see the flashing red light? *(Okay, there was no real light but you get it.)* Before you get far away from your pillow, did you look up? Did you know that someone has been up along with an angel watching over you? Yep! There is someone who hears and cares who is beyond us.

You need not deal with life speculatively all the time. There is a God who listens. He listens out for you, and he listens to you. He has some things to share with you that will ready you for the day if you pause to get the report. Life can get you in a hurry and the most important things get neglected.

Why do I say this today? Well, I feel someone may be where I have been, and I pray you will not stay as long. You may feel that you need to make what is needed happen by yourself, but not so! You need not live and function alone.

God cares for you. He knows your thoughts and dreams. He wants you to share them with him even while you brush your teeth, shower, get dressed or drink that first cup of coffee. He loves fellowship with you and will even ride with you as you hit the road for business, school or errands. His word says that he is with us even to the end of the world.

He it with you meaning He is right beside you. If you

do not believe He is, just call Him. Go ahead! Tell Him, "I am waiting." Okay, enough! There is no greater love and no better friend. Open your heart and mind today. Slow your roll and incorporate him in your time. He has been waiting for you to rise all night. Your appointment is on God's calendar. Just show up. He expects you. Much Love!

Abiding Love
Day 19

Good Morning,

Learn to appreciate a variety of dress styles and person styles. We do not all look alike nor dress alike. What may be totally uncomfortable and unappealing to me may be the thing that you are and wear best. It is not good to judge people based on your comfortability level nor is it fair for others to judge you as such.

Find your place and settle into it. If others are not comfortable there, do not judge them or dislike them for it. Approval is important, but not at the expense of identity. Many seek it and fear losing it. Some think they can never get it from you. Be willing to accept others for who they are. It may not be who you would be or want them to be but give yours. Embrace them as an individual and not as an idea. Many have killed themselves out of a fear of rejection or that they can win no one's approval. Many live isolated because they feel they are not approved of.

Accept others where they are and without attempting to change them to a personal mold. Someone may live another day because you chose to accept them. Also, take the time to introduce them to your extra special self and give them the opportunity to know the true you. I mean it! Quit looking like you playing. Be "coo-a-see-cra-tiv-an-qui-it" *(cool secretive and quiet).* Have a great day! Much Love!

Abiding Love
Day 20

Good Morning,

This is a "No Frown Day." Nobody is going out with a torn up face. Corners of the mouth will not point south, and ugly expressions are forbidden upon such pretty and handsome faces. You cannot just get your hair right. You have to put on more than eye makeup, lipstick, cologne or perfume. You need to wear more than nice jewelry. You need to prepare your smile today.

That's right! Get those teeth gleaming and turn up the corners of your mouth. A smile is like the sun...warm and welcome. People reach out to you when you smile and avoid you when you don't. Have you ever seen a Cheshire cat? It always looks like it is having a good time or up to something. The depiction is of a cat that might even seem to have too many teeth in its mouth and cannot help but smile. Turn yours on.

I believe the cat found that a meow was not a good response to God for all that he has done. Therefore, it embarked upon a devastating smile and kept brushing his teeth too *(Smile maintenance...I wonder if Cheshire cats use mouthwash)*. Think of all you have to be grateful for and the love God has for you. Think of all the living you can live and everything that goes into it. The Rap world had Busta Rhyme, but you will be known as Busta Smile. Have a great day. Much Love!

"And we have known and believed that God has loved us. God is love, and he who abides in love abides in God and God in him" ~ I John 4:6

Abiding Love
Day 21

Good Morning

I have a question. Ready? Have you ever said, "People just get on my nerves?" Be honest! Do not say it aloud, and no one will know, but me and you. Still quiet? Okay, let me confess. I have. In fact, I have made some noise about it in the car and been caught by a few folks behaving in an extremely animated fashion. With emphasis, I have said, "People get on my nerves!" At times, they really do. In traffic, nerves are often stomped on. Some people can be so rude! At times, I have wanted to smack someone *(extreme road rage)* until I thought that many of them are feeling just like me.

Sometimes, I am aggravated. I have found myself speaking Sunday school words unapproved by Heaven *(Don't tell the saints)*. My actions take concern for no others. Then, while huffing and puffing and being distracted, I make a mistake, and someone shoots me the look I just shot someone else. I wonder what is wrong with them, and then God whispers in my ear the law of reciprocity: "You shall reap what you sow"

I forget that if everyone who feels like me will act like me and treat me the way I am treating others, we will all be in bad places. Listen, we all get in a hurry and upset with each other, but rather than be angry and vindictive, let us understand as we would seek to be understood. Everybody deserves a break, and everybody needs to strengthen the nerves others get on because we get on other's nerves sometimes also. Family, friends, co-workers, and others may do a little damage, but that is okay. We need other people just as they are even as they need us in all of our imperfections. Share a little more grace. Be a little more patient. Thank God for so many yet good nerves that when folks get on a few of them it is alright. Much Love!

Abiding Love
Day 22

Good Morning,

I am not asking this question for me. I am asking for you to consider. What do you want? That sounds simple enough, but is it really? What do you sincerely want? Often, we feel we are clear when we really are not. God asks that question of us and then says, "Huh?" "If I was not omniscient, I would have no clue what you mean."

What does it take to get what you want? What are you willing to become to accommodate what you want? How can God shape you to fit or handle what you want? What can you give up or be willing to have added? Where are you willing to go and why do you want it? Have you pondered it all? Do you really want it?

Ask and search yourself. Often God says, "Yes", but we fail to follow through *(at least I do)*. I find myself asking God for answers he has already given. Because it doesn't happen like I thought, I think he does not want me to be or have it. God sends many more short memos than he does long answers. I believe God likes a little graffiti because he left a note on the wall for King Belshazzar and sends voices messages from Heaven as he did with Jesus. Nothing is too big, too small or too difficult. He wants you to be open to him and use both your faith an imagination. Great faith will give you the ability to make audacious requests.

Listen for God and tell him what is on your mind for

real. Neither you nor I can blow His mind. When you find out, you will really go for it or allow it to happen. The operative word is REALLY. The question is not, *"What will you settle for?* But *what do you really want?"*Jesus is waiting on your request. Much Love!

Abiding Love
Day 23

Good Morning...

Let's grant permission today. It is okay to cry sometimes. The saying that big boys and girls do not cry should be stricken from all vocabulary. What are we to do with these tears if not from time to time shed them? Crying is healthy and necessary. Crying is good.

There are times when crying is the only expression you have. Never think that because you cry, you are weak. Sometimes, we cry because we are happy. Sometimes, we cry because something was hilarious. Sometimes we are in pain and hurting when we cry. Sometimes mourning and sadness lead us to cry. Sometimes something in the environment irritates our eyes. Your tears may be for you and sometimes you shed them for others. Shed them when you must. Do not damage your eyes trying to hold tears in and wind up with a "bubble face." Release them when you must. Big boys and big girls DO cry for a number of reasons. So be big when you must.

Crying, whether of joy or sorrow, reveals that you can be touched. Tears show that you can feel and be moved. Crying reveals a sensitive spirit; "Jesus Wept." Even if they were talking behind his back, Jesus would not have been upset if he was called a Water Head or Water Bucket. He wept over Lazarus. He wept over Jerusalem, and He wept over his plight in the Garden of Gethsemane. He did so with no shame, and He is God. Be as He is free to be that same way. A good cry is good for the soul. Much Love!

Abiding Love
Day 24

Good Morning,

I had a dog once. It was a nice but ordinary dog. He was not the next Scooby Doo, Lassie or Benji. He was just a dog. He was a yard dog. I would pick on him and call him a mutt. It did not seem to bother him. He seemed to smile and take it as a compliment. In my mind, I know I heard my plain old ordinary mutt say, "thank you" and then call me a mutt. I said "What?" He said, "Woof, woof, Bow wow, dude," which means "You are a real mutt dude."

My dog walked off kind of snooty knowing he had made a stinging point that I had yet to get. I felt insulted and inspired to withhold the dog food until I thought of what it means to be a mutt. Often, I have used it as a derogatory term, but it actually means to be a mix. It means to be a blend. It means that the blood and genes of multiple ethnicities flows in my veins. It means I am like a beautiful living quilt. It means I am within myself what humanity is to be in community.

I asked a veterinarian friend of mine about mixed breeds and he spoke of *(1) Sheepadoodle: Old English Sheepdog and Poodle, (2) Pomsky:Pomerian and Husky (3) Cavapoo: Cavalier King Charles Spaniel and Poodle, (4) Puggle: Pug and a Beagle , (5) Labradoodle: Labrador Retriever and a Poodle, and (6) Pomchi: Pomeranian and a Chihuahua.* They are all mixed breeds. They are endearing and expensive mutts.

If America is true to its creeds, we become a mutt nation. Great churches are mutts. Great neighborhoods are mutts. Great schools are mutts. It is all in how you define it and say it. Wow! This dog may be on to something. He keeps smiling because he knows it. I am proud to know that no matter your makeup, you can be proud of who you are. Take pride in your heritage and culture. Because someone speaks of you in an insulting manner does not mean it defines you. Let's go out and get along. Have an uncontrollably wonderful day. Much Love!

Abiding Love
Day 25

Good Morning...

How many times have you heard this from your parents? You need to eat your vegetables. How many times have you said it to your children? Eat what is good for you! If you said, "but I do not like them," parents would say, "Eat them because they are good for you!" They meant it. My dad would share that food was cheaper than medicine and we did not need to *"root hog and die poor."* My mom assured us that we would learn to both appreciate and eat what was put before us. They understood that the first benefit of eating was not pleasure, but nourishment. Food gave us fuel for strength and health. They did not yield to our dietary choices and requests

I am glad they did not and that I followed in their footsteps with my children. They would sometimes get the pouting mouth and take much time to do what was required, but eventually and under the persuasion that there would be no desert without veggies, they yielded. So it is with not only food issues, but also life issues. It is imperative to understand that often what is best for us may not be what we like most. Healthy, spiritual, and physical nourishment requires things that do not always please or excite our taste, but are necessary to intake. Too much candy, sugar, chip and sodas will rot teeth and ruin a waistline. Vegetables will bless them inside and out. Fruit and exercise do a body good. Prayer and faith grow your spirit. Worship, study and service build relationship.

Can I get a witness? *(It sounded like a good spot for a little preaching invitation).* Let's be about it today. Determine to take more of what is good for us. We may not love the taste as much as the other stuff, but be assured, it is best, and we will be able to celebrate the results. Much Love!

Abiding Love
Day 26

Good Morning,

Let us pray radically today. Search yourself, and see what's not done that you asked God to help you do. Take all those things out of the closet, and lay them before God. They are still good. They are just not completed. These may be some doosies that you dared pray when you felt the Spirit of the Lord moving upon you; then got off to yourself and said, "I have got to be crazy!" However, you were not. Let's get some floor on our knees *(Well, only if you can get down like that. Otherwise, sitting up is fine.)* Let's really get God's attention.

I have some great things to do that sound overwhelming. They are bigger than I and cannot be accomplished without faith in God, determination and focus. I need some encouraging words and prayers from you that will make the task easier. I am here to say, "I need you." I need to be here for you. In fact, we need each other. We are better walking together and working together. We challenge each other to move beyond the mundane and superficial. We dream aloud and speak truth to God when we do so together.

I pray that extraordinary things will manifest themselves today. Yes I pray things with that *"Boom Baby"* impact will happen! I pray the angels that attend to us will say, "Lord, you need to see what they are praying today!" Look beyond the mediocre and see more. Expect more. We do not need to get lucky. Let's posture ourselves and ask to be blessed. Just pray. Do it for me! I am doing the same for you. Have a great day. Much love!

Abiding Love
Day 27

Good Morning,

It is inventory time. Check yourself out. Do you like what you see? Aww, Sookie Sookie now! *(Can you say that in a devotional? If not, we will edit it in the second edition.)* It is said of us that we are fearfully and wonderfully *made (Psalm 39:14).* Are you still checking yourself out? Show me what you are working with! Okay, well just show yourself. Guess what? The easiest thing to find as you do this is what is wrong or imperfect and not the best stuff.

It is easy to speak of what is bad with your life, but the real question is "what is good with it?" It is amazing that there can be 1,000 feet of clean wall with 3 small dark smudges and many will give more attention to the smudge *(what is wrong)* than the clean portions of the wall *(what's right).* Is that you? If it is, do not do this in your life. See the good stuff. Even the basic Booga Bear person *(yes, I said, "Booga Bear!")* has good to be seen. Maybe, you have had a bad day or made some mistakes. Maybe you have gotten some things wrong. It is okay! Reflect on the number of times you have gotten it right. See the unmarred portions of the wall.

You will never be happy if you never see what is good in your life. Had a bad week? You are handling it and it's coming to an end. That's good. Got up on the wrong side of the bed? You can get back in and get out on the right side. That is good. The fact that God gave you another day to live makes it a good thing. Yes! *(Doing

my happy dance) Take it from here. Start counting and write it down. Move beyond smudges and give Him praise. Celebrate the good in your life today. Smudges can be removed.
Much Love!

Abiding Love
Day 28

Good Morning,

Take your shot! What shot you may ask? Take the one that you have been thinking of but not taken yet. Take your shot. Stop dribbling! Quit passing it up! Stop giving the opportunity to someone else. You have the ball and cannot just hold it. You have practiced and readied yourself. Take the shot. The moment is yours. The goal is before you. Expectation is high that you will make it. You are trusted with the ball.

What if you miss? Follow up! Take another shot. What if it gets blocked? Learn to shoot around and through obstacles. What if it is not pretty? There are no points given for style. Life is not about perfections, and it is not reasonable to assume you will make every shot that way. The object is to be certain you take a good one. Your good shot that may be missed provides those around you who are not the best shooters to rebound and score on put-backs. Life and sports are at their best when you are on a team.

Do not be afraid. Do not distrust yourself. God has given you this day to score. He dished it to you when he awakened you this morning. You have the ball. Take a good shot. Remember: a missed shot can be redeemed but a missed opportunity cannot. Take it! Booyah! Have a great day. Much Love!

Abiding Love
Day 29

Good Morning,

Get ready to take the stage. Every day you have a role and though it may not always be a starring role, it is yours to live. You cannot linger in obscurity. You were chosen for this. God auditioned you in the womb and cast you for right now. Prepare to live the role assigned to you as you go out today. God has brought you to this moment for such a time as this.

The objective is not to amaze the audience or silence the critics, but to be true to the person and purpose you were assigned. Take the stage! You cannot be effective living in daily rehearsal and hiding offstage. You cannot give another your life role to live. Step forward. No one can live your life like you. God wrote the script and the director has no one else to be cast that will bring the character power and ability to do this like you.

Whether others cheer, boo, or seem unimpressed by you, does not matter. Do not be overwhelmed by any of this. There is a greater audience taking notice. Every day will not be your best, but seek to make every day better. You cannot relive yesterday, and tomorrow is another scene in your life story. Today's scene will prepare you for it so live your best life today. Lights! Camera! Action! You are on. Have a great day. Much Love!

Abiding Love
Day 30

Good Morning...

Here is something for you to say to you. Are you ready? Here it is: *"I am deeper than what is seen. I cannot be comprehended by my leaves, branches or even fruit. To really know me you must know my roots. I am deep."* This is a confession that needs to be made every day. It is a truth that you need to declare. It is a reality to never be forgotten or forsaken in the midst of adversity or criticism.

Circumstances may affect you, but do not think that because you are sometimes shaken by the winds of life that you are neither stable nor strong. You are deeper than your appearance. You are rooted. You are here to stay. You are a force extracting from your sown place, giving life from your being, drawing energy from the atmosphere, and bearing fruit that nurtures those who take time to know you. You must tell yourself this.

Yes! This is a declaration or testament to be made every day and to be expressed to anyone who says, *"You know I know you."* They may have known who you have been, but every day, you are emerging, conforming more to the image of God, and on the anvil, being perfected in Him, by Him and for Him. Be amazed at His work in you and on you. Every day say, "Lord, do it!"

Remember this, *"I am deeper than what is seen and greater than circumstances that confront me. Rattling my leaf does not destabilize my roots."* That deserves a resounding AMEN! Now, in the words of my dad, mom, and many of your relatives like them, you may say to the naysayers, *"Put that in your pipe and smoke it."* Have a deep rooted happy day. Much Love!

"And now abides these three things Faith, hope and love. But the greatest of these is love"
I Corinthians 13:13

Abiding Love
Day 31

Good Morning,

Be Fruitful! Multiply! Replenish! It is amazing that this is one of the first commandments given. It implies to be actively engaged in sowing, cultivating and increasing who and what we presently represent. The implication is that more is in us that may come forth with a little work. The last of the command says, "...and multiply and replenish the earth." You and I are responsible to invest and supply our community and world with the best of who God has made us. He wants more of you. Isn't that amazing? Think of it. God wants you to increase for the benefit of the world in which you live.

Be careful. You want to be certain you sow the good person you are minus avoidable deficiencies. You and I are going to reproduce seed according to whom and what we are. This cannot happen by yourself. Just as we share the fruit of ourselves we need others to sow into us and cultivate us. We need good environment and refreshing. We need to draw strength from and share it with others. We need this to be the most fruitful US possible.

For example, an apple tree will not reproduce bananas. Its seed renders it impossible. Grapes will not bring forth peaches nor watermelons or apples. What you are is what you bring forth. God commands you to sow you. That is the most amazing thing you have. It is your best gift. This is not about babies *(Otherwise there would be some untouched folk in great number)*. It is about giving and receiving the best of another and becoming more than you ever could alone. Give your best knowing that who you are and what you give is what you will get back. Be fruitful! He said it. Let's do it. Much Love!

Abiding Love
Day 32

Good Morning,

I asked a young lady, "Why do you not come to Church?" She replied, "I have been hurt too many times at church. I do not think you should get that from God's people; therefore, I just worship God alone and leave people alone. God knows my heart." Do you understand? Without hesitation I blurted out "No! I did not mean to be insensitive to her experience but the words seemed in a rush to address her question. The words "despised, rejected, wounded, hated and sorrow" came to my mind, and I said, "NO" again.

I said, "You have no right to quit on what God has not quit on and He is not giving you a pass and private audience. You do not quit on spouse, children, parents, work, or other social engagements when you get disappointed. You and I have failed and hurt ourselves more than anyone else ever could, yet we live with ourselves. You have no right to quit on neither God nor His people. Besides, how many times have you let Him down? You get no pass. Get back involved with the imperfect people He has perfected by His blood. You are precious. You are vital and unique. You are chosen and no one can do what God has gifted you to do. If you are his, he requires it of you." Is she you?

Perhaps this word is for you regarding your church, family or other important people. The family needs you to come home. Presence is important. My parents used to say teeth and tongue may fall out sometimes but they stay in the same mouth. Remember, you are who they are, and they are you. You have a right to feel and even become frustrated, but never a right to quit. God wants his children together. Go home. The family needs you. Have a great day. Much Love!

Abiding Love
Day 33

Good Morning,

Let's appreciate a dad today. Do you know why? No, not because it's Father's Day. It is just because fathers are special. Without them, we miss a great part of our essential community. They are that strong and protective presence that help hold everything together. They are made in the image of God and imitators of how he takes care of his children.

Sometimes we miss the value of them because we just do not give them the necessary consideration. No doubt mothers are truly essential and to be cherished but not to the point that the presence and value of a father is diminished. The awesome fact is that no matter whom or what I am and become 50% of that is an investment he made in me and 50% is what my mom gave me *(stop thinking the right eye looks like dad and the left knee like mom)*. Dads love, care and share. Sometimes, they appear strong and invincible, but beneath the covering also exists a man who feels and sacrifices. There is a man forever proud of his children. There is a man who needs to know that his children value and celebrate him. If no one else does, he needs that from his own.

That is you and me. That is us. All that he is and leaves in the heart finds its breath in us. Give your dad a big shout out whether he is here or in glory. He needs to hear it from you. Make his day! "Daddy, I praise God for giving you to me, and I thank you for teaching through the Love you gave me!" To the Ultimate Father above give love, honor and praise. "Father God, with Gratefulness, I lift you up and Bless your Majestic Name for your "So" Love - Hallelujah!" Have an "ab-ba-do-shus" *(Daddy Love day).* Much Love!

Abiding Love
Day 34

Good Morning,

Years ago there was a song entitled, "I'll Always Love my Mama;" it says, "She's my favorite girl." It captures the sentiment of so many of us. There is no one in the world like mama. She is the one who brings us forth and helps bring us up. She loves lifts and leads. She bandages our wounds, wipes tears, extends apron strings and has eyes under the hair in the back of her head. They throw shoes around corners at fleeing children. They are better than police and ferment into mellow, gentler Gigis, Nanas and Grandmothers *(Bigma has just faded into history)*.

Where I grew up we had many Mamas. There was your own mama. There were grandmothers, aunty mamas, other mamas, play mamas, God mamas, church mamas, mama nem's, school mamas, teacher mamas and many more. It took every one of them to bring us through, and we are better people because of them. Let us applaud all who make this motherhood special for us. My mom was my angel. I never could have made it without her. She poured so much into me and so consistently, that I thought it had always been there. She loved me, and when I asked what I could give her to show my appreciation, she simply asked me to love her back.

Gifts and flowers are good to share, but take time from your schedule to share with your mom some of that great child she birthed and reared. Do not hurriedly express your gratitude to God. Share with Him and them what they have done, still do, and mean in this life. God bless you. Much Love!

Abiding Love
Day 35

Good Morning...

Do you remember how exciting it was to see a cake being made by hand? Mama called it beating a cake, but I guess it sounded so violent, they changed it to mixing. But the mixer had beaters because we never called them mixing tools and well...Mom would do a majestic work on that cake. She would buy the best of stuff and follow all the great baking protocols: measuring without measuring spoons and inventing words to describe how much she was using.

All ingredients would be gathered and put into one bowl and mixed *(beaten)* until there was a smooth mix that did not leave any one ingredient standing out. In the mixing *(beating)* they sacrificed individuality for the sake of becoming a blended whole. They departed from labels and wrappers to live a life in a bowl. They went through a blending *(beating)* process and endured the fires of an oven that help to make them one. You could see the unity they had while recognizing the contribution of each ingredient. They did not mix in the bowl but blended. They became one. They became a cake.

That is the essence of true integration and unity. This applies to any relationship that would be more than basic. Find what you want that requires a shedding of labels an inclusion of others. We need to learn to blend and live in a healthy and thriving oneness. You were never meant to live life alone. Get in the bowl. You do not need to take a beating but you sure would be a great part of an excellent blend.   Much Love!

Abiding Love
Day 36

Good Morning,

All things point up. That is your reference point for this morning. Why? It is because God made them that way. Although we bow in reverence we lift our eyes and hands up to honor and reverence Him. He is our origin, our creator, and sustainer. He is above all, in all and through all. He comes down that we might go up and be with him forevermore.

We are not our own point of reference nor are we our ultimate destiny. Our origins are deeper than our first, and our death shall not be the end of our existence. Wow! I think I really said something! God watches over us at all times and wants you to know that in all your days and situations, He is there. Look up! More than the sky is above. Whatever issues you may have, look up. Whatever prayers, praise or predicaments you may have, look up. Do not let yourself get down. He keeps his eyes on you.

I assure you there is no friend like Jesus. He who watches sparrows looks even closer at you. Take a deep breath, and raise a hand today; no matter where you are or what you are doing, He is present and has you covered. Phenomenal is the order for your day. I just heard Him say, "Let's Go!" Much Love!

Abiding Love
Day 37

Good Morning,

A great issue that has to be dealt with is the issue of clutter. Yes! Well, maybe not in your life, but in mine it has been a challenge. I have a lot of good stuff that has been with me for a number of years. It takes up a lot of space. Sometimes, it is quite unorganized, but it is mine. I love it and that is it. I work around it. I live in it. It makes me comfortable. I give it rule in my home, my car and even in my heart. It dominates my time and energy because it is very demanding.

This is not good because many of my prayers have been answered, but God could not give me what I asked for because there was no place to put it. I did not want to give up what had always been there or I was so busy tending to the things that have always been that I could not receive the blessing of the new.

When space and life become overcrowded, and time is exhausted on everything that has been to the extent that you have no time for what God has for the days to come, you have become a victim of clutter. It does not matter whether it is good clutter or bad clutter; you must deal with it. A cluttered closet, a cluttered mind, a cluttered heart and a cluttered spirit jeopardizes your life.

Ask yourself if what is taking place in your life is functional and purposeful. If it has no place in your attention or agenda, it may be time to get rid of it. If you do more for it than it does for you, it may be time to get rid of it. If its shelf life has expired and does not fit any longer, it is time to rid yourself of it. You may have become as I have been: a prisoner of my own clutter. It is time to break out and make room for new blessings and opportunities. They may be just around the pile. Much Love!

Abiding Love
Day 38

Good Morning,

Relationships take time if they are to function at their best. It is good to have them but they require time. They require investment, maintenance and repair. They evolve and change. They require of you effort and engagement that increases as it grows. They never need less but can become less without the proper attendance. They cry out and distance sets in without time spent. Other things and people get in the way or take up space not because they mean you harm but the space they settle in has been vacant for so long they did not know that it was taken and the even sadder part is that you may not have even known they or it was there.

So what do you do then? How do you make your relationships strong again? Another question to ask of today is, "how am I taking care of my most important relationships?" You may even need to ask those you are in relationship with whether it is God, spouse, children, friends, or co-workers how you are doing. That sounds a bit risky, but it is so very necessary. You might feel you are doing an excellent job only to discover you have been missed or that the relationship is suffering because of what has not gone into it for a long time or even from the quality of what it has been given.

Listen friend. You need the people in your life in a big way. The best of life is spent in relationship. Hug more, laugh, give and celebrate. Talk and interact.

Connect and engage. Stop just being around and get involved. Prioritize the most important things and people. They need you as you do them. Much Love!

Abiding Love
Day 39

Good Morning,

When it is time to say goodbye, prepare yourself and do so in a manner befitting the person who has gone away. Death is never easy for those who remain because it means those who have filled a vital place in our lives are no longer there. We feel the vacated space, and it just does not seem right. It hurts to know that it will never be as it always has been and all that remains is a shell of what has been.

Inevitably, we all must leave, and others will feel about us that way we have felt about others. Since we know these things, let us take the following steps to prepare to say goodbye. First, cherish the time you have right now. Make the best of it. Second, appreciate that person and tell them so. Value what they bring to your life and treat it as treasure. Third, celebrate that person. Birthdays, anniversaries, special occasions, made up days, just because moments are important and empowering. Fourth, create moments and memories. Take pictures and begin to recall times you have shared while you are living. Do it with that one and do it even when they are not in the room. When that person departs they will not leave you alone. The moments and memories you share will be embedded in your soul.

Understand this friend; every goodbye is just on the other side of hello. Whether it is parent, child, spouse or friend, there will be departures. Life leads to death and death for the faithful is but the door to eternity that we must walk through. Make your mark on those you love and allow them to do the same to you. Goodbye should not take you by surprise. Do not check out today and certainly, do not rush anyone else off the scene, but pack a bag of life and memories to leave for them and recognize the one filled with the same they have prepared for you. Much Love!

Abiding Love
Day 40

Good Morning,

Muhammad Ali made a frequent pronouncement to the world that he was the greatest of all time. He boisterously filled the ears of opponents often infuriating them and creating a desire to knock his head from his shoulders. Ali used it as incentive. It gave him and edge, and then he would interject more poetry and rhymes while proceeding to call the round of that opponent's demise and accomplishing it. His proclamation was strong and backed up.

However, there is a greater proclamation and a greater fighter than Ali. No, it is not Jack Johnson, Rocky Marciano, Joe Louis, Floyd Patterson or Sugar Ray Robinson. It is Love. Solomon declares love is as strong as death (Song of Solomon 8:6). Jesus says that God so loved the world that he gave his only begotten Son that whosoever believes in him shall not perish but have eternal life (John 3:16). Again, Jesus admonishes us to abide in his love (John 15:9), and Paul makes the pronouncement in 1 Corinthians 13, "Now abides these three, faith, hope and love, but the greatest of these is love."

Love is the greatest thing that exists. The love of God for humanity is the greatest thing we can receive. Our love for each other ought to be given with all strength and effort. It ought to grow and abide with others even as we abide in the love of the Father and the Son. Love holds us accountable to loving. It feeds, feels, and fertilizes. It keeps when all else lets go and sustains as Nothing else will. It pursues and protects. It helps and heals. It relieves, rescues, and never takes a day off. It says we will get through this even when we see no way through. It creates life and remains after death. It may be rejected cannot be killed. It governs all that is and is what God desires most from his children. It is eternal. It shall ever abide. I just wanted to give you a heads up. Have a phenomenal day. Much Love!

"…and lo I am with you always, even unto the end of the world" ~ Matthew 28:20

Books by Vernon Lloyd

Dear Church People

So You want to be a Preacher?

So You Want to be a Leader?

I was Just Thinking I

I was Just Thinking II

Cross Talk

Shall the Cross go Unclaimed?

Back in the Day

Mama's Songs Series

Contact Information

Vernon Lloyd
Veedeelloyd@gmail.com

Shaunta Ellis
Sellis1284@Pineland.net

Made in the USA
Columbia, SC
17 June 2024